**SCHOLASTIC**

# Comprehension Skills
## 40 Short Passages for Close Reading

### GRADE 2

Linda Ward Beech

New York • Toronto • London • Auckland • Sydney
Mexico City • New Delhi • Hong Kong • Buenos Aires

*Teaching Resources*

The reading passages in this book were selected and adapted from the following titles in the series, Reading Passages That Build Comprehension: *Compare & Contrast*, *Context Clues*, *Fact & Opinion*, *Inference*, *Main Idea & Details*, and *Predicting*. (Scholastic, 2005). Copyright © 2005 by Linda Ward Beech.

Cover design by Jorge J. Namerow
Interior design by Jason Robinson
Illustrations by Mike Gordon

ISBN: 978-0-545-46053-8
Text copyright © 2012 by Linda Ward Beech
Illustrations copyright © 2012 by Scholastic Inc.
Published by Scholastic Inc.
All rights reserved.
Printed in the U.S.A.

21    40    24 23 22

# Contents

## Passages

# Using This Book

Reading comprehension in nonfiction involves numerous thinking skills. Students require these skills to make sense of a text and become successful readers. This book offers practice in key skills needed to meet the Common Core State Standards in Reading/Language Arts for grade two. (See page 6 for more.) Each student page includes a short passage focusing on three of these essential comprehension skills.

## Comprehension Skills At-a-Glance

Use the information that follows to introduce the reading comprehension skills covered in this book.

### Main Idea & Details

Understanding the main or key idea of a paragraph is crucial for a reader. The main idea is what the paragraph is about. The other parts of the paragraph help to explain more about this key idea. Sometimes, the main idea is in the first sentence of a paragraph.

The information that supports the main idea is usually referred to as the details. Details help a reader gain a fuller understanding of a paragraph.

### Context Clues

Using context means determining an unfamiliar word's meaning by studying the phrases, sentences, and overall text with which the word appears. Context clues help readers comprehend and enjoy a text and also read more smoothly and efficiently.

### Compare & Contrast

Recognizing how events, characters, places, and facts are alike and different helps a reader gain a richer understanding of a text. Sometimes a reader can learn more about something by finding out what it is *not* like than what it is like. A comparison shows similarities, while a contrast shows differences.

In this paragraph, students have to read the entire text and ask themselves, "What is this paragraph mainly about?" The main idea is supported by different facts about Mercury.

In this example, other words in the paragraph provide a context for comprehending the word *pests*.

## Predict

Good readers take time to think about a text. One way they do this is by thinking ahead to determine what may happen next or how an event will unfold. Often, information a reader has come across in the text provides clues to what will happen next. In many cases readers also use what they already know when they make predictions.

## Inference

Although most primary students don't know what an inference is, many are most likely making inferences—both in their daily lives and when reading—without being aware of it. Students should understand that writers don't include every detail in their writing; it is up to readers to supply some information. A reader makes a guess or inference by putting together what is in a text with what he or she already knows. Inferring makes a significant difference in how much a reader gains from a text.

## Fact & Opinion

Readers who can identify and differentiate between statements of fact and opinion are better able to analyze and assess a text. Students should learn to recognize phrases, such as *I think* and *you should*, that signal opinions.

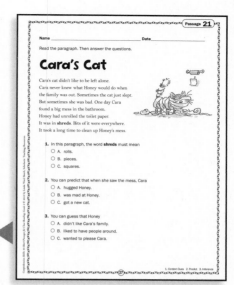

The writer never says that the cat likes to have people around, but information in the paragraph plus what readers already know helps make it a likely guess.

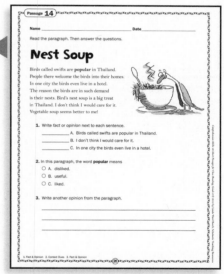

To appreciate this story, the reader should understand that the writer has shared several opinions as well as some facts about the bird's nest soup.

## Tips

★ Tell students to first read the passage and then answer the questions. Show them how to fill in the circles for bubble-test questions.

★ The comprehension skills targeted in the questions accompanying each passage are labeled at the bottom of the page.

★ Review the completed pages with students on a regular basis. Encourage them to explain their thinking for each correct answer.

# Meeting the Common Core State Standards

The passages and comprehension questions in this book are designed to help you meet both your specific English/Language Arts standards and learning expectations as well as those recommended by the Common Core State Standards Initiative (CCSSI). The activities in this book align with the following CCSSI standards for grade two.

## Reading Standards for Literature

**Key Ideas and Details**
1. Ask and answer such questions as *who, what, where, when, why,* and *how* to demonstrate understanding of key details in a text.
3. Describe how characters in a story respond to major events and challenges.

**Craft and Structure**
5. Describe the overall structure of a story, including describing how the beginning introduces the story and the ending concludes the action.

**Integration of Knowledge and Ideas**
7. Use information gained from the illustrations and words in a print text to demonstrate understanding of its characters, setting, or plot.

**Range of Reading and Level of Text Complexity**
10. By the end of the year, read and comprehend literature, including stories, in the grades 2–3 text complexity band proficiently, with scaffolding as needed at the high end of the range.

## Reading Standards for Informational Text

**Key Ideas and Details**
1. Ask and answer such questions as *who, what, where, when, why,* and *how* to demonstrate understanding of key details in a text.
3. Describe the connection between a series of historical events, scientific ideas or concepts, or steps in technical procedures in a text.

**Craft and Structure**
4. Determine the meaning of words and phrases in text relevant to a *grade 2 topic or subject area.*
6. Identify the main purpose of a text, including what the author wants to answer, explain, or describe.

**Integration of Knowledge and Ideas**
8. Describe how reasons support specific points the author makes in a text.

**Range of Reading and Level of Text Complexity**
10. By the end of the year, read and comprehend informational texts, including history/social studies, science, and technical texts, in the grades 2–3 text complexity band proficiently, with scaffolding as needed at the high end of the range.

## Reading Standards: Foundational Skills

**Fluency**
4. Read with sufficient accuracy and fluency to support comprehension.
   a. Read on-level text with purpose and understanding.
   c. Use context to confirm or self-correct word recognition and understanding, rereading as necessary.

## Language Standards

**Knowledge of Language**
3. Use knowledge of language and its conventions when writing, speaking, reading, or listening.

**Vocabulary Acquisition and Use**
4. Determine or clarify the meaning of unknown and multiple-meaning words and phrases based on *grade 2 reading and content,* choosing flexibly from an array of strategies.
   a. Use sentence-level context as a clue to the meaning of a word or phrase.
5. Demonstrate understanding of word relationships and nuances in word meanings.
   b. Distinguish shades of meaning among closely related verbs.
6. Use words and phrases acquired through conversations, reading and being read to, and responding to texts.

**Name** _____ **Date** _____

Read the paragraph. Then answer the questions.

# Rob's Job

The Dells had a big fireplace. On snowy winter days they often lit a fire. Rob's job was to make sure there was plenty of wood to burn. He would take his sled to the woodshed. There he loaded logs onto the sled. Then he would **haul** the wood back to the house and bring it in to burn.

**1.** In this paragraph, the word **haul** must mean
- ○ A. chop.
- ○ B. pull.
- ○ C. burn.

**2.** The main idea of this paragraph is
- ○ A. why Rob had a sled.
- ○ B. snowy winter days.
- ○ C. getting wood for a fireplace.

**3.** How do you think the Dells feel about their fireplace?

_____

_____

_____

1. Context Clues   2. Main Idea   3. Inference

Name _____ Date_____

Read the paragraph. Then answer the questions.

# A Gardener's Friend

What do ladybugs eat? Their main food
is a tiny insect called an aphid.
Most gardeners think of aphids as **pests**.
These insects cause harm to plants
by sucking out their juices.
When people see ladybugs in their gardens,
however, they are pleased.

**1.** Which sentence tells what most likely happens next?

○ A. Gardeners will get rid of the ladybugs.

○ B. The ladybugs will eat the aphids.

○ C. The aphids will attack the ladybugs.

**2.** In this paragraph the word **pests** must mean

○ A. troublemakers.

○ B. plants.

○ C. helpers.

**3.** How are ladybugs and aphids different?

_____

_____

_____

**Name** _____ **Date** _____

Read the paragraph. Then answer the questions.

# A Tale of Tails

Pigs are known for having curly tails.
They're so cute! Experts say that you can tell
how healthy a pig is by the curl of his tail.
A pig with a curly tail is in good health.
But a pig with a straight tail is not. Poor pig.
A straight tail on a pig is a sign of illness.
Farmers should take good care of their pigs
so they don't get sick.

**1.** Write *fact* or *opinion* next to each sentence.

_____ A. They're so cute!

_____ B. Experts say that you can tell how healthy a pig is
by the curl of its tail.

_____ C. A straight tail on a pig is a sign of illness.

**2.** Which sentence is most likely true?

○ A. Pigs like to wag their tails.

○ B. Pigs always get sick.

○ C. Farmers check their pigs' tails often.

**3.** What will a farmer most likely do if a pig's tail is straight?

_____

_____

_____

Name _____ Date _____

Read the paragraph. Then answer the questions.

# A Mark on the Wall

Anna took off her shoes. She stood straight
with her back against the wall. Anna's mother
put the ruler on Anna's head and made a little mark
on the wall. It was two inches above another mark.
Next to the new mark, Anna's mother wrote the date.
"Wow!" she said. "No wonder your jeans are too short."

1. Which sentence is most likely true?
   ○ A. Anna's mother is measuring Anna's head.
   ○ B. Anna's mother is mad at Anna.
   ○ C. Anna has grown two inches taller.

2. You can guess that the next mark will be
   ○ A. the same.
   ○ B. lower.
   ○ C. higher.

3. Most likely Anna's mother will
   ○ A. buy Anna new jeans.
   ○ B. give Anna old jeans.
   ○ C. make Anna stop growing.

1. Inference  2. Predict  3. Predict

**Name** _____  **Date** _____

Read the paragraph. Then answer the questions.

# Meet Mercury

Can you name the planets in our solar system?
Mercury is one of them. Like the other planets,
Mercury moves in a path around the Sun.
Mercury travels faster than the other planets.
It speeds along at about 107,000 miles an hour.
Mercury is the planet closest to the Sun.
Its days are very hot, and its nights are very cold.
There is no water on Mercury.

**1.** The main idea of the paragraph is

  ○ A. the lack of water on Mercury.

  ○ B. the planets in the solar system.

  ○ C. what the planet Mercury is like.

**2.** A detail that tells more about the main idea is

  ○ A. the speed at which Mercury travels around the Sun.

  ○ B. the names of the other planets in the solar system.

  ○ C. how fast other planets in the solar system travel.

**3.** Write one way that Mercury differs from other planets.

_____

_____

_____

1. Main Idea   2. Details   3. Compare & Contrast

Name _____ Date _____

Read the paragraph. Then answer the questions.

# Ellen's Saturday

When Ellen wakes up on Saturday,
there is snow on the ground.
Ellen **races** through her breakfast.
Then she pulls on a hat, jacket, and gloves.
Her boots are not in the closet,
so she runs outside in her sneakers.
She joins her friends to go sledding.

**1.** Which sentence tells what most likely happens next?

   ○ A. Ellen's feet will get cold and wet.

   ○ B. Ellen will lose her sled on the hill.

   ○ C. Ellen's friends will take off their boots.

**2.** You can tell that Ellen loves

   ○ A. breakfast.

   ○ B. snow.

   ○ C. boots.

**3.** In this paragraph, the word **races** means

   ○ A. rushes.

   ○ B. drags.

   ○ C. runs.

1. Predict   2. Inference   3. Context Clues

**Name** _____ **Date** _____

Read the paragraph. Then answer the questions.

# School Zoo

Many classrooms have pets. This is the best
way for students to learn about animals.
But classroom pets need a place to go
during the summer. In Plano, Texas, the schools
have a mini-zoo. Teachers can **borrow** pets
for the school months. When summer comes,
they return the pets to the zoo. Schools in
other towns should follow this example.

**1.** Write *fact* or *opinion* next to each sentence.

_____ A. This is the best way for students to learn about animals.

_____ B. In Plano, Texas, the schools have a mini-zoo.

_____ C. Schools in other towns should follow this example.

**2.** You can guess that

○ A. the pets dislike being in the classroom.

○ B. there is no school in the summer.

○ C. the zoo closes in the summer.

**3.** In this paragraph, the word **borrow** means

○ A. have forever.

○ B. have for awhile.

○ C. pay money for.

Name _____ Date _____

Read the paragraph. Then answer the questions.

# Birds and Turtles

Mother birds lay eggs in nests where they are safe. Little birds hatch from the eggs. They cheep and cheep until their parents bring them food. Turtles lay eggs, too. Mother turtles lay their eggs in the sand where the eggs will be safe. But mother turtles cover the eggs and leave. When it is time, small turtles **hatch** from the eggs. They dig their way up and learn to find food on their own.

1. How are birds and turtles alike?
   - ○ A.  They have hard shells.
   - ○ B.  The young hatch from eggs.
   - ○ C.  The mothers leave the eggs.

2. How are birds and turtles different?
   - ○ A.  Bird parents feed their young.
   - ○ B.  They lay eggs in safe places.
   - ○ C.  The young need food to eat.

3. In this paragraph, the word **hatch** means
   - ○ A.  opening on a roof.
   - ○ B.  make a plan.
   - ○ C.  come out of.

Name _____ Date _____

Read the paragraph. Then answer the questions.

# A Smart Fish

Fred was a very smart fish. He lived in
a peaceful river. Nothing much happened
there unless people came around.
Then Fred had to be **alert**.
A yummy worm might mean a trap.
If Fred wasn't careful, he could end up as someone's supper.
He had seen it happen to many careless fish.

**1.** In this paragraph, the word **alert** must mean

  ○ A.  watchful.

  ○ B.  careless.

  ○ C.  sleepy.

**2.** You can guess that a worm Fred saw might be

  ○ A.  on a fishing pole.

  ○ B.  in the ground.

  ○ C.  on a water lily.

**3.** If Fred saw a worm, you can predict he would

  ○ A.  eat it quickly.

  ○ B.  swim away.

  ○ C.  try to save it.

1. Context Clues  2. Inference  3. Predict

Name _____ Date_____

Read the paragraph. Then answer the questions.

# Horse Helpers

Horses are wonderful helpers for humans. In some cities the police ride horses to control large crowds. Cowboys use horses to help round up herds of cattle. In some countries farmers still use horses to pull plows or wagons. People also use horses to carry them from place to place.

1. The main idea of the paragraph is
   ○ A. the different jobs that horses can do.
   ○ B. how the police use horses in crowds.
   ○ C. the ways that animals help people.

2. A detail that tells more about the main idea is
   ○ A. how cowboys use horses in their work.
   ○ B. the kinds of horses used in police work.
   ○ C. the names of countries using farm horses.

3. Write *fact* or *opinion* next to each sentence.
   _____ A. Cowboys use horses to help round up herds of cattle.
   _____ B. Horses are wonderful helpers for humans.
   _____ C. People also use horses to carry them from place to place.

1. Main Idea  2. Details  3. Fact & Opinion

**Name** _____ **Date**_____

Read the paragraph. Then answer the questions.

# Kinds of Leaves

The leaves on trees are not all alike.
Some leaves have jagged edges called teeth.
Toothed leaves can be oval, skinny,
or shaped like a heart. Beech and elm trees
have such leaves. Other trees have leaves
shaped like a hand with the fingers spread out.
These leaves have three to seven fingers,
also called lobes. Many maple trees have such leaves.
Both types of leaves drop off trees in the fall.

1. How are toothed leaves and hand-shaped leaves alike?
   - ○ A. They grow on trees.
   - ○ B. They have lobes.
   - ○ C. They have teeth.

2. How are toothed leaves and hand-shaped leaves different?
   - ○ A. Maple leaves drop off in the fall.
   - ○ B. Elm leaves are shaped like hands.
   - ○ C. Toothed leaves have jagged edges.

3. The main idea of this paragraph is
   - ○ A. trees have different kinds of leaves.
   - ○ B. maples trees have hand-shaped leaves.
   - ○ C. beech trees have jagged edges.

Name _____ Date_____

Read the paragraph. Then answer the questions.

# Raisin Capital

California is the raisin capital of the world.
Farmers there begin by growing grapes.
When the grapes are **ripe**, workers pick them
from the vine. Then the grapes are laid out in
California's dry, sunny air. The grapes begin
to get wrinkled as they lose their water.
They change color, too.

**1.** Which sentence tells what most likely happens next?

○ A. The grapes get moldy and rotten.

○ B. Farmers water the dry grapes.

○ C. The grapes turn into raisins.

**2.** You can guess that grapes grow well because

○ A. they grow on vines.

○ B. of California's dry, sunny air.

○ C. California is the raisin capital.

**3.** In this paragraph, the word **ripe** means

○ A. wrinkled.

○ B. picked.

○ C. full-grown.

1. Predict  2. Inference  3. Context Clues

**Name** _____ **Date** _____

Read the paragraph. Then answer the questions.

# Ship of the Desert

Do you know what a ship of the desert is?
It is a camel. These animals are good
for carrying people and supplies across hot,
dry deserts. Camels can go many days
without getting thirsty. Camels can also go
for a long time without food. They live off the fat
in their humps when there is no food.

1. Which sentence is most likely true?
   - ○  A.  Camels eat sand most of the time.
   - ○  B.  Camels don't like to eat or drink.
   - ○  C.  The desert has little food or water.

2. You can guess that some trips camels make
   - ○  A.  take many days.
   - ○  B.  are in cold places.
   - ○  C.  are across the sea.

3. After a camel crosses a desert, you can predict that it
   - ○  A.  isn't very hungry.
   - ○  B.  drinks a lot of water.
   - ○  C.  acts like a ship.

1. Inference  2. Inference  3. Predict

Name _____ Date_____

Read the paragraph. Then answer the questions.

# Nest Soup

Birds called swifts are **popular** in Thailand.
People there welcome the birds into their homes.
In one city the birds even live in a hotel.
The reason the birds are in such demand
is their nests. Bird's nest soup is a big treat
in Thailand. I don't think I would care for it.
Vegetable soup seems better to me!

1. Write *fact* or *opinion* next to each sentence.

   _____ A. Birds called swifts are popular in Thailand.

   _____ B. I don't think I would care for it.

   _____ C. In one city the birds even live in a hotel.

2. In this paragraph, the word **popular** means

   ○ A. disliked.

   ○ B. useful.

   ○ C. liked.

3. Write another opinion from the paragraph.

   _____

   _____

   _____

1. Fact & Opinion   2. Context Clues   3. Fact & Opinion

**Name** _____ **Date** _____

Read the paragraph. Then answer the questions.

# Using Plants

Long ago, people used plants to make
colorful dyes. They boiled plants in water.
Different plants gave off different colors.
For example, boiled acorns made a light brown,
and beets made a bright pink. The skins from
certain onions made an orange-colored dye.
Once the **dyes** were ready, people dipped wool
or other cloth into them.

1. In this paragraph, the word **dyes** must mean
   ○ A. stops living.
   ○ B. colorings.
   ○ C. foods.

2. A good title for this paragraph would be
   ○ A. Colors From Plants.
   ○ B. Pink From Beets.
   ○ C. Orange From Onions.

3. You can guess that today
   ○ A. vegetables are never used in dyes.
   ○ B. there are other ways to dye cloth.
   ○ C. dyes are not as colorful as long ago.

1. Context Clues  2. Main Idea  3. Inference

Name _____ Date_____

Read the paragraph. Then answer the questions.

# Beatrix Potter

Beatrix Potter (1866–1943) loved animals.
She also loved to draw. As a young girl she
kept a sketchbook of plants and family pets.
She became a student of nature. Later on,
Beatrix Potter wrote stories for children.
The main characters were animals.
Perhaps you have read *The Tale of Peter Rabbit*
or *Squirrel Nutkin.*

1. The main idea of the paragraph is
   ○ A.  Beatrix Potter's interest in nature.
   ○ B.  the titles of Beatrix Potter's books.
   ○ C.  the names of Potter family pets.

2. A detail that tells more about the main idea is
   ○ A.  how Beatrix Potter learned to draw.
   ○ B.  what Potter drew in her sketchbook.
   ○ C.  how the book *Squirrel Nutkin* ends.

3. You can guess that Beatrix Potter
   ○ A.  read her stories to pets.
   ○ B.  drew the pictures for her stories.
   ○ C.  wrote stories about plants.

Name _____ Date_____

Read the paragraph. Then answer the questions.

# Two Apples

Apples all grow on trees, but they are not
the same. A Cortland apple is bright red with
green **streaks**. It is quite juicy. Cortlands are good
for eating fresh and for cooking. People often
use them in salads, too. Another red apple
is the Red Delicious. It also has green streaks.
The Red Delicious apple is heart-shaped
and has five knobs on the bottom.
People eat this apple fresh.

**1.** How are Cortland and Red Delicious apples alike?

  ○ A. They are used for cooking.

  ○ B. They are heart-shaped.

  ○ C. They are red in color.

**2.** How are Cortland and Red Delicious apples different?

  ○ A. The Red Delicious apple is heart-shaped.

  ○ B. The Cortland apple is eaten fresh.

  ○ C. The Red Delicious apple has green streaks.

**3.** In this paragraph, the word **streaks** means

  ○ A. blobs.

  ○ B. spots.

  ○ C. lines.

1. Compare & Contrast   2. Compare & Contrast   3. Context Clues

Name _____ Date _____

Read the paragraph. Then answer the questions.

# Night Life

Most people do their sleeping during the day.

But many wild creatures do not.

Mice do much of their roaming at night.

It's harder for foxes to hunt them in the dark.

When otters live near people, they are more active

at night. A dragonfly **sheds** its skin at night.

It takes a few hours for the new adult's wings to grow strong.

By morning the dragonfly is ready to fly away.

**1.** Which sentence is most likely true?

○ A. Otters like to live near people.

○ B. It is safer for some animals at night.

○ C. Wild animals have more fun at night.

**2.** Write one way that otters and mice are alike.

_____

_____

**3.** In this paragraph, the word **sheds** means

○ A. loses.

○ B. grows.

○ C. eats.

**Name** _____ **Date** _____

Read the paragraph. Then answer the questions.

# Animals of the Arctic

Animals of the Arctic have different ways
of staying safe. Each summer the snowshoe
hare's fur is brown. It is hard for enemies
to see the hare on the brown land of the Arctic.
But winter is coming. It will soon snow.
The hare's thick fur will change color to help
keep it safe.

**1.** Which sentence tells what most likely happens next?

○ A. The hare's coat will become white.

○ B. The hare's enemies will see it in the snow.

○ C. The Arctic snow will turn brown.

**2.** You can guess that the snowshoe hare has thick fur because winters

○ A. are brown in the Arctic.

○ B. are cold in the Arctic.

○ C. are white in the Arctic.

**3.** The main idea of the paragraph is

○ A. how winter affects Arctic animals.

○ B. how summer affects Arctic animals.

○ C. how Arctic animals stay safe.

1. Predict  2. Inference  3. Main Idea

**Name** _____ **Date** _____

Read the paragraph. Then answer the questions.

# Dolls Inside Dolls

Nesting dolls are sets of wooden dolls. I think they are very cute. You twist open each doll to find another, smaller doll inside. These dolls were first made in Russia in 1890. Today major league baseball teams are handing out these dolls. They are called Stackable Stars. Each doll is painted to look like a player on the team. Many fans collect the dolls.

**1.** Write *fact* or *opinion* next to each sentence

_____ A. I think they are very cute.

_____ B. Today major league baseball teams are handing out these dolls.

_____ C. Many fans collect the dolls.

**2.** Another good title for this paragraph would be:

○ A. Painted Dolls

○ B. Nesting Dolls

○ C. Dolls for Fans

**3.** Write another fact from the paragraph.

_____

_____

_____

**Name** _____ **Date**_____

Read the paragraph. Then answer the questions.

# Cara's Cat

Cara's cat didn't like to be left alone.
Cara never knew what Honey would do when
the family was out. Sometimes the cat just slept.
But sometimes she was bad. One day Cara
found a big mess in the bathroom.
Honey had unrolled the toilet paper.
It was in **shreds**. Bits of it were everywhere.
It took a long time to clean up Honey's mess.

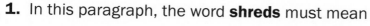

1. In this paragraph, the word **shreds** must mean
   - ○ A. rolls.
   - ○ B. pieces.
   - ○ C. squares.

2. You can predict that when she saw the mess, Cara
   - ○ A. hugged Honey.
   - ○ B. was mad at Honey.
   - ○ C. got a new cat.

3. You can guess that Honey
   - ○ A. didn't like Cara's family.
   - ○ B. liked to have people around.
   - ○ C. wanted to please Cara.

1. Context Clues  2. Predict  3. Inference

Name _____   Date_____

Read the paragraph. Then answer the questions.

# Marc Brown

Marc Brown writes books about an aardvark
named Arthur. Many of Brown's characters
are based on people in his life. For example,
Buster is based on a childhood friend.
So is the character Sue Ellen. Two other characters,
D.W. and Francine, are like his sisters in many ways.
Another great book character is Grandma Thora.
She is named for Marc Brown's real grandmother.

1. The main idea of the paragraph is
   - ○ A.  how Marc Brown started writing the Arthur books.
   - ○ B.  why Marc Brown's books have so many characters.
   - ○ C.  where Marc Brown's characters come from.

2. A detail that tells more about the main idea is
   - ○ A.  who Francine is based on.
   - ○ B.  why Arthur is an aardvark.
   - ○ C.  where Marc Brown grew up.

3. Write an opinion from the paragraph.

_____

_____

_____

**Name** _____ **Date** _____

Read the paragraph. Then answer the questions.

# Frogs and Toads

People often confuse frogs and toads.
Both are amphibians. This means they are cold-blooded;
their temperature stays the same as their surroundings.
Frogs and toads have four legs and no tails.
They use their back legs for jumping.
The legs on frogs are longer. Toads have drier,
lumpier skin. Most adult frogs live in or near water.
Most **adult** toads live on land.

1. How are frogs and toads alike?
   - ○ A. They live mostly on land.
   - ○ B. They are cold-blooded.
   - ○ C. They have long tails.

2. How are frogs and toads different?
   - ○ A. Toads jump with their back legs.
   - ○ B. Toads live mostly on land.
   - ○ C. Frogs have lumpier skin.

3. In this paragraph, the word **adult** means
   - ○ A. grown-up.
   - ○ B. young.
   - ○ C. cold-blooded.

1. Compare & Contrast   2. Compare & Contrast   3. Context Clues

Name _____ Date_____

Read the paragraph. Then answer the questions.

# News in the Past

Long ago there was no TV. No one had a radio.
There were no computers. And there were very
few newspapers. How did people get news?
One way was from a town crier. This person
walked through the streets and called out
the news. If something special happened,
the town crier beat a drum or rang a bell.
People would run to hear the news.

**1.** Which sentence is most likely true?

○ A. There were few ways to get news long ago.

○ B. Most news in the past appeared in print.

○ C. In the past, people weren't interested in news.

**2.** The main idea of this paragraph is

○ A. running to hear the news.

○ B. how people got news long ago.

○ C. no TV, radio, or computers.

**3.** Write one way that getting news today is different from the past.

_____

_____

_____

1. Inference   2. Main Idea   3. Compare & Contrast

Name _____ Date_____

Read the paragraph. Then answer the questions.

# From Canada to Mexico

The monarch butterfly is quite a traveler.
Each spring the monarch leaves Mexico.
It starts flying north to Canada. On the way,
it dies. But its young **continue** north.
These butterflies also die, but their young go on.
This continues until fall. Then the great-great-grandchild
of the first butterfly turns and heads south.

1. Which sentence tells what most likely happens next?
   ○ A.  The young butterfly will get lost.
   ○ B.  The young butterfly will fly east.
   ○ C.  The young butterfly will head for Mexico.

2. In this paragraph, the word **continue** means
   ○ A.  keep going.
   ○ B.  return.
   ○ C.  stop to rest.

3. Another good title for this paragraph would be
   ○ A.  Flying North.
   ○ B.  Butterfly Travels.
   ○ C.  Monarchs in Mexico.

1. Predict  2. Context Clues  3. Main Idea

Name _____  Date_____

Read the paragraph. Then answer the questions.

# Shape of a Plate

Once, home plate on a baseball field was square. Then, in 1900, the shape was changed. Since then home plate has had five sides. That's so **weird**. The reason for this change was to help umpires. They find it easier to see the ball with this five-sided shape. It seems to me they still have trouble seeing the ball at times. I think the players also have problems.

1. Write *fact* or *opinion* next to each sentence.

   _____ A. Once, home plate on a baseball field was square.

   _____ B. That's so weird.

   _____ C. It seems to me they still have trouble seeing the ball at times.

2. In this paragraph, the word **weird** means
   ○ A. wonderful.
   ○ B. strange.
   ○ C. cool.

3. Write another opinion from the paragraph.

   _____

   _____

   _____

**Name** _____ **Date** _____

Read the paragraph. Then answer the questions.

# Remembering Stories

The earliest people did not have a written language. Instead, people learned things by telling and listening to stories. How did storytellers recall everything? Some drew pictures on cave walls to help them remember. Some made up chants to the **rhythm** of drums. Other storytellers made belts or necklaces. Colored threads, beads, and special knots stood for different events.

**1.** The main idea of the paragraph is
- ○ A. long-ago drawings on cave walls.
- ○ B. why there were no books or magazines.
- ○ C. different ways storytellers recalled events.

**2.** A detail that tells more about the main idea is
- ○ A. which people became storytellers.
- ○ B. beads on belts helped recall things.
- ○ C. what kinds of stories people told.

**3.** In this paragraph, the word **rhythm** means
- ○ A. rocking.
- ○ B. singing.
- ○ C. musical beat.

1. Main Idea  2. Details  3. Context Clues

Name _____ Date _____

Read the passage. Then answer the questions.

# Don's Flower

Don's class was learning about plants.
The teacher asked the students to bring in a flower.
Don chose a pretty flower from his mother's garden.
"How will I get this to school?" he asked.
"The flower will **wilt** on the bus."
Don's mother showed him what to do. She wrapped
a wet paper towel around the flower stem. "This will keep
your flower alive until you can put it in water," she said.

1. In this paragraph, the word **wilt** must mean
   - ○ A. spill over.
   - ○ B. lose freshness.
   - ○ C. grow slowly.

2. The main idea of this paragraph is
   - ○ A. how Don kept his flower fresh.
   - ○ B. studying flowers in school.
   - ○ C. wrapping a stem in a paper towel.

3. You can predict that Don
   - ○ A. lost his flower on the bus.
   - ○ B. brought a flower to school every day.
   - ○ C. got his flower to school without wilting.

**Name** _____ **Date**_____

Read the paragraph. Then answer the questions.

# Whales in Water

Whales live all their lives in water.
These large mammals are very smart.
The blue whale is the biggest mammal of all.
Both it and the humpback whale are baleen whales.
They have no teeth. Instead they have baleen,
or thin plates, in their mouth to strain out food.
The humpback whale is black with white on it.
This whale has long flippers. The blue whale
is a blue-gray color.

1. How are blue whales and humpback whales alike?
   - ○ A. They are black and white.
   - ○ B. They have long flippers.
   - ○ C. They are both mammals.

2. How are blue whales and humpback whales different?
   - ○ A. The humpback is a baleen whale.
   - ○ B. The blue whale is very smart.
   - ○ C. The blue whale is larger.

3. Which sentence is most likely true?
   - ○ A. Whales eat each other.
   - ○ B. Whales get their food from the ocean.
   - ○ C. Whales eat baleen.

**Name** _____   **Date** _____

Read the paragraph. Then answer the questions.

# A Busy Cactus

A giant cactus grows in the desert.
By the time the cactus is 150 years old,
it is full of holes. In one hole lives a bat.
Another hole is home to some insects.
Birds lay eggs and **raise** families in the cactus, too.
Even some pack rats find a place to live
in the cactus. When one animal leaves the cactus,
another one moves in.

**1.** The main idea of this paragraph is
- ○ A. a giant cactus that is 150 years old.
- ○ B. a giant cactus that is a home for animals.
- ○ C. people make holes in a giant cactus.

**2.** Which sentence is most likely true?
- ○ A. The animals are harmful to the cactus.
- ○ B. Baby birds live in the cactus.
- ○ C. Only flying animals live in the cactus.

**3.** In this paragraph, the word **raise** means
- ○ A. lift up.
- ○ B. throw out.
- ○ C. bring up.

Name _____ Date _____

Read the paragraph. Then answer the questions.

# Pumpkins in History

In the 1600s, Native Americans such as
the Pequot planted pumpkins in their cornfields.
The big pumpkin leaves helped to keep
the soil **damp** and free from weeds.
Native Americans also used pumpkins for food
and medicine. The English colonists were surprised.
They thought pumpkins were only fit for animals.
But the colonists had little food; they were hungry.

1. Which sentence tells what most likely happens next?

   ○ A. The colonists get sick from eating pumpkins.

   ○ B. The colonists begin to raise and eat pumpkins.

   ○ C. The Native Americans stop eating pumpkins.

2. At first the English colonists differed from Native Americans because

   ○ A. the colonists used pumpkins for medicine.

   ○ B. the colonists thought pumpkins were only for animals.

   ○ C. the colonists kept the soil damp with pumpkin leaves.

3. In this paragraph, the word **damp** means

   ○ A. clean.

   ○ B. dry.

   ○ C. wet.

1. Predict  2. Compare & Contrast  3. Context Clues

Name _____ Date_____

Read the paragraph. Then answer the questions.

# Corn Maze

A family in Virginia plants a field of corn
in the pattern of a maze. The pattern for the maze
is designed on a computer. Then family members
use the maze map to make paths in the field.
They plant the corn around the paths.
By July the maze is ready for visitors.
It covers 15 acres! Visitors enjoy trying
to walk through it. If people get lost,
they hold up a flag for help.

1. The main idea of the paragraph is
   - ○ A. how computers are used for mazes.
   - ○ B. how a cornfield becomes a maze.
   - ○ C. why it's fun to walk through a maze.

2. A detail that tells more about the main idea is
   - ○ A. mazes have a long history.
   - ○ B. some people plant gardens as mazes.
   - ○ C. the corn maze is ready in July.

3. Which sentence is most likely true?
   - ○ A. Family members wait in the maze.
   - ○ B. It's hard to get through the maze.
   - ○ C. Visitors use a computer to get through the maze.

Name _____ Date_____

Read the paragraph. Then answer the questions.

# Firehouse Dogs

Dalmatians are known as firehouse dogs. They are wonderful dogs. They are fast and have good memories. Dalmatians also get along well with horses. Long ago, fire trucks were pulled by horses. Firefighters used Dalmatians to run ahead of the trucks and clear a path. Today some firehouses still keep a Dalmatian. They no longer have to run ahead of horses, though.

**1.** Write *fact* or *opinion* next to each sentence.

_____ A. Dalmatians are known as firehouse dogs.

_____ B. Long ago, fire trucks were pulled by horses.

_____ C. They are wonderful dogs.

**2.** Which sentence is most likely true?

○ A. Fire trucks have other ways to clear a path today.

○ B. Dalmatians still help fight fires.

○ C. Some firehouses still keep horses.

**3.** Write another fact from the paragraph.

_____

_____

_____

1. Fact & Opinion   2. Inference   3. Fact & Opinion

**Name** _____ **Date** _____

Read the paragraph. Then answer the questions.

# Pigs and Bears

Two popular tales for children are "The Three Little Pigs" and "The Three Bears." Both are about three animals. The bears all live in the same house. The pigs each have their own house. The pigs have problems with a wolf. He destroys two of their houses. The bears have trouble with a girl named Goldilocks. She breaks a chair and eats their porridge.

1. How are the stories alike?
   - ○ A. They are about some pigs.
   - ○ B. Goldilocks breaks a chair.
   - ○ C. They are about three animals.

2. How are the stories different?
   - ○ A. The pigs have three houses.
   - ○ B. The tales are both popular.
   - ○ C. The animals have a problem.

3. Which sentence is most likely true?
   - ○ A. Pigs are more popular than bears.
   - ○ B. Houses appear in all children's stories.
   - ○ C. Children enjoy animal stories.

**Name** _____ **Date** _____

Read the paragraph. Then answer the questions.

# Cabin Cleanup

The cabin had been closed up all winter.
Inside, it was dim and **gloomy**. Spiderwebs
hung in the corners. Dust covered the floors.
Mia said, "Let's make this place more cheerful."
She opened the wooden shutters to let in light.
Then she began sweeping and dusting.
Soon the cabin would be ready for summer fun.

1. In this paragraph, the word **gloomy** must mean
   ○ A. dark.
   ○ B. clean.
   ○ C. cheery.

2. Which sentence is most likely true?
   ○ A. Mia is not alone.
   ○ B. Mia is lonely.
   ○ C. Mia is by herself.

3. You can predict that
   ○ A. the cabin will be sold next winter.
   ○ B. the cabin will be closed next winter.
   ○ C. the cabin will be closed all summer.

1. Context Clues  2. Inference  3. Predict

Name _____ Date_____

Read the paragraph. Then answer the questions.

# Staying Warm

How do clothes keep you warm?
Clothes keep you from losing body heat.
That's because clothes trap air.
The heat from your body cannot
get through the air. Snow works
in the same way. It traps lots of air.
People lost in winter storms sometimes dig
holes in the snow. This helps them keep warm.

1. Which sentence is most likely true?
   ○ A. People need layers of clothing in summer.
   ○ B. People wear layers of clothing in cold places.
   ○ C. People use snow to keep cool in summer.

2. The main idea of this paragraph is
   ○ A. how to stay warm in winter storms.
   ○ B. kinds of clothes to wear in winter.
   ○ C. trapping body heat to stay warm.

3. Write one way that clothes and snow are alike.

   _____

   _____

   _____

**Name** _____ **Date**_____

Read the paragraph. Then answer the questions.

# Dolphin Teamwork

Dolphins usually work together as a team.
They like to travel in groups.
Large groups are called herds.
Smaller groups are known as pods.
If a dolphin is sick, others in the pod
will swim alongside of it.
They help the sick dolphin get
to the water's surface so it can breathe.
Dolphins also work together to find food.
And when a mother dolphin looks for food,
others will care for its baby.

**1.** The main idea of the paragraph is
   ○ A.  how dolphins work together.
   ○ B.  helping out mother dolphins.
   ○ C.  how dolphins act with people.

**2.** A detail that tells more about the main idea is
   ○ A.  what dolphins do at school.
   ○ B.  different kinds of dolphins.
   ○ C.  how dolphins travel in groups.

**3.** Which sentence is most likely true?
   ○ A.  Dolphins fight among themselves.
   ○ B.  It would be unusual to see a lone dolphin.
   ○ C.  Dolphins often get sick.

1. Main Idea  2. Details  3. Inference

Name _____ Date _____

Read the paragraph. Then answer the questions.

# On the Food Trail

People often come across ants on sidewalks.
Scientists say that there is a reason for this.
People **tend** to drop food and food wrappers on sidewalks.
These people are slobs. They should know better.
Ants are always looking for food. If a scout ant
finds food on a sidewalk, it leaves a trail for other ants.
Soon there are lots of ants following the trail.

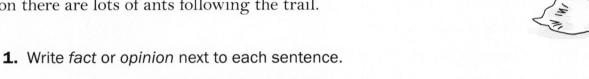

1. Write *fact* or *opinion* next to each sentence.

   _____ A. These people are slobs.

   _____ B. People tend to drop food and food wrappers on sidewalks.

   _____ C. They should know better.

2. The main idea of this paragraph is
   - ○ A. why ants are on sidewalks.
   - ○ B. how ants follow people around.
   - ○ C. why people are slobs.

3. In this paragraph, the word **tend** means
   - ○ A. rarely do.
   - ○ B. never will.
   - ○ C. are likely to.

1. Fact & Opinion   2. Main Idea   3. Context Clues

**Name** _____ **Date** _____

Read the paragraph. Then answer the questions.

# Thanksgiving Customs

Americans have celebrated Thanksgiving
for hundreds of years. Today people eat turkey
and squash just like long ago. However,
people use forks today. In colonial times
people used spoons, knives, and their fingers.
Often there was only one cup.
It was passed around the table.
Since there were few chairs in colonial times,
children often stood while eating.
But people used napkins long ago, just as they do today.

1. How was Thanksgiving long ago like Thanksgiving now?

   ○ A.  People had only one cup at dinner.

   ○ B.  People had napkins then and do now.

   ○ C.  Children stood at the table to eat.

2. How was Thanksgiving long ago different from Thanksgiving now?

   ○ A.  People did not have forks in the past.

   ○ B.  People still eat turkey and squash.

   ○ C.  People had their meal at a table.

3. Which sentence is most likely true?

   ○ A.  People used paper napkins long ago.

   ○ B.  Children got tired standing at meals long ago.

   ○ C.  People weren't thirsty long ago.

1. Compare & Contrast   2. Compare & Contrast   3. Inference

Name _____ Date_____

Read the passage. Then answer the questions.

# Setting the Table

It was Joe's **chore** to set the table for supper.
Each night he put out dishes and silverware
for four people. One day Joe got a phone call.
That night he set the table for six people.
His sister teased him. "Can't you count?" she asked.
But then the doorbell rang. It was Grandma and Grandpa.
"Good job, Joe," said Mom.

**1.** In this paragraph, the word **chore** must mean
- ○ A. choose.
- ○ B. job.
- ○ C. count.

**2.** Which sentence is most likely true?
- ○ A. Joe's grandparents called him.
- ○ B. Joe's sister went out for dinner.
- ○ C. The grandparents came for dinner every night.

**3.** Which sentence tells what most likely happens next?
- ○ A. Joe's grandparents spent the night.
- ○ B. Six family members ate dinner together.
- ○ C. Mom asked Joe to make the dinner.

# Answers

**page 7:**
1. B
2. C
3. Answers will vary but should reflect the text.

**page 8:**
1. B
2. A
3. Possible: They eat different things.

**page 9:**
1. A. Opinion
   B. Fact
   C. Fact
2. C
3. Possible: They will get treatment if the pig is sick.

**page 10:**
1. C
2. C
3. A

**page 11:**
1. C
2. A
3. Possible: It travels faster.

**page 12:**
1. A
2. B
3. A

**page 13:**
1. A. Opinion
   B. Fact
   C. Opinion
2. B
3. B

**page 14:**
1. B
2. A
3. C

**page 15:**
1. A
2. A
3. B

**page 16:**
1. A
2. A
3. A. Fact
   B. Opinion
   C. Fact

**page 17:**
1. A
2. C
3. A

**page 18:**
1. C
2. B
3. C

**page 19:**
1. C
2. A
3. B

**page 20:**
1. A. Fact
   B. Opinion
   C. Fact
2. C
3. Vegetable soup seems better to me!

**page 21:**
1. B
2. A
3. B

**page 22:**
1. A
2. B
3. B

**page 23:**
1. C
2. A
3. C

**page 24:**
1. B
2. They are more active at night.
3. A

**page 25:**
1. A
2. B
3. C

**page 26:**
1. A. Opinion
   B. Fact
   C. Fact
2. B
3. Possible: They are called Stackable Stars.

**page 27:**
1. B
2. B
3. B

**page 28:**
1. C
2. A
3. Another great book character is Grandma Thora.

**page 29:**
1. B
2. B
3. A

**page 30:**
1. A
2. B
3. Answers will vary.

**Page 31:**
1. C
2. A
3. B

**page 32:**
1. A. Fact
   B. Opinion
   C. Opinion
2. B
3. I think the players also have problems.

**page 33:**
1. C
2. B
3. C

**page 34:**
1. B
2. A
3. C

**page 35:**
1. C
2. C
3. B

**page 36:**
1. B
2. B
3. C

**page 37:**
1. B
2. B
3. C

**page 38:**
1. B
2. C
3. B

**page 39:**
1. A. Fact
   B. Fact
   C. Opinion
2. A
3. Answers will vary.

**page 40:**
1. C
2. A
3. C

**page 41:**
1. A
2. A
3. B

**page 42:**
1. B
2. C
3. Possible: They trap air and keep your body warm.

**Page 43:**
1. A
2. C
3. B

**page 44:**
1. A. Opinion
   B. Fact
   C. Opinion
2. A
3. C

**page 45:**
1. B
2. A
3. B

**page 46:**
1. B
2. A
3. B